Food

CARROTS

Louise Spilsbury

Heinemann Library
Chicago, Illinois

Designed by Celia Floyd
Illustrated by Alan Fraser
Originated by Ambassador Litho
Printed in Hong Kong/China by South China Printing Co.

06 05 04 03 02
10 9 8 7 6 5 4 3 2 1

Library of Congress Cataloging-in-Publication Data
Spilsbury, Louise.
  Carrots / Louise Spilsbury.
     v. cm. -- (Food)
Includes index.
Contents: What are carrots? -- Kinds of carrots -- In the past -- Around the world -- Looking at carrots -- Planting carrots -- Growing carrots -- Digging carrots -- Carrots to us -- Eating carrots -- Good for you -- Healthy eating -- Carrot soup recipe.
  ISBN 1-58810-616-0 (HC),
  1. Cookery (Carrots)--Juvenile literature. 2. Carrots--Juvenile literature. [1. Carrots.] I. Title. II. Series.
  TX803.C35 S65 2002
  641.6'513--dc21

2002000467

Acknowledgments
The author and publishers are grateful to the following for permission to reproduce copyright material: pp. 4, 21, 23, 28 (left and right), 29 (top and bottom) Liz Eddison; pp. 5, 11, 14, 16, 19 Holt Studios International; p. 6 Thompson and Morgan (UK) Ltd; pp. 7, 10, 24, 25 Corbis; pp. 8, 9 Bridgeman Art Library; p. 12 Corbis; pp. 13, 20 Imagebank; p. 15 Martin Caunce/P. Caunce and Son; p. 17 Stone; p. 18 FPG International; p. 22 Trevor Clifford.

Cover photograph: Gareth Boden.

Every effort has been made to contact copyright holders of any material reproduced in this book. Any omissions will be rectified in subsequent printings if notice is given to the publisher.

Some words are shown in bold, **like this.** You can find out what they mean by looking in the glossary.

Contents

What Are Carrots?

Carrots are a kind of **vegetable.**
A vegetable is a part of a plant you
can eat. You can eat carrots **raw**
or cooked.

Carrots grow on carrot plants. You cannot see carrots growing. They are a part of the plant that grows under the ground.

Kinds of Carrots

Carrots come in many sizes, shapes, and colors. There are fat, small, long, and thin carrots. There are red, white, yellow, and purple kinds.

Most people eat long orange carrots. They were first grown in the Netherlands more than 400 years ago. Now they are popular all over the world.

In the Past

The **Ancient Romans** believed that eating carrots made stomachaches better. They also thought carrots helped them to see at night.

Carrots became popular in the rest of Europe about 500 years ago. Most people ate the carrots. Some decorated their hats with the feathery leaves!

Around the World

Carrots grow best in places where it is not too hot and not too cold. This farmer in Ecuador grows carrots for her family to eat.

This huge carrot farm is in California. Some of the carrots grown here are sold in United States. Others are **exported** to other countries.

Looking at Carrots

Carrots grow from **seeds.** In the soil, the seeds start to grow. **Shoots** grow upwards towards the light. **Roots** grow down into the soil.

Carrots are a kind of root. As they grow down into the soil, they get fatter and longer. Tall, fluffy leaves form on the shoots.

Growing Carrots

Carrots grow best in loose soil. That is why farmers use a **plow** to break up the soil before they put the **seeds** into the ground.

This farmer is using a machine called a planter. It drops seeds into the soil. It spaces the seeds out so that the plants have room to grow.

Spraying and Digging

Farmers need to protect carrot plants from **diseases** and **pests.** Some farmers put special sprays on the plants to keep them from being **damaged.**

When the carrots are big enough to eat, farmers dig them up. They use a machine that pulls up the carrot plants. It also cuts off the leaves.

Washing and Checking

A truck takes the carrots to a **packing house.** The carrots go into a machine that cleans them. Water washes the soil off the carrots.

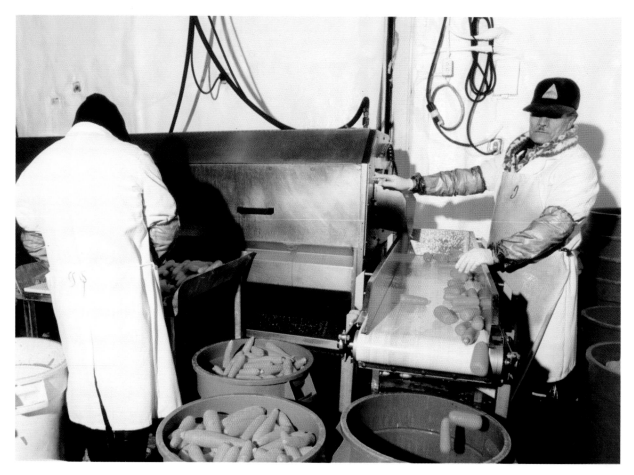

The carrots then go onto a **conveyor belt.** Workers check them and throw away any carrots that are bad, split, or broken.

Carrots to Us

A machine sorts the carrots into different sizes. They are moved in large crates, bags, or boxes. Finally, trucks take the carrots to grocery stores.

Some carrots are sold with the leaves on. Other carrots are **frozen** or packed into cans with salt and water. These keep longer than fresh carrots.

Eating Carrots

Many people cut the skin off carrots before they eat them. Others eat the skin, too. You should wash carrots well before you eat them.

Carrots are used in dishes like soups, stews, cakes, and salads. Carrots are also used to make food **products** such as carrot juice.

23

Good for You

Carrots contain a lot of **vitamin** A. This vitamin helps to keep your skin and bones healthy. It also helps your body fight **disease.**

Carrots also contain **fiber**. Fiber
is a part of some foods that passes
through your body when you eat it.
It helps keep your body healthy.

Healthy Eating

The food guide **pyramid** shows how much of each different kind of food you should eat every day.

All of the food groups are important, but your body needs more of some foods than others.

You should eat more of the foods at the bottom and the middle of the pyramid. You should eat less of the foods at the top.

Carrots are in the **vegetable** group. Your body needs three servings of vegetables each day.

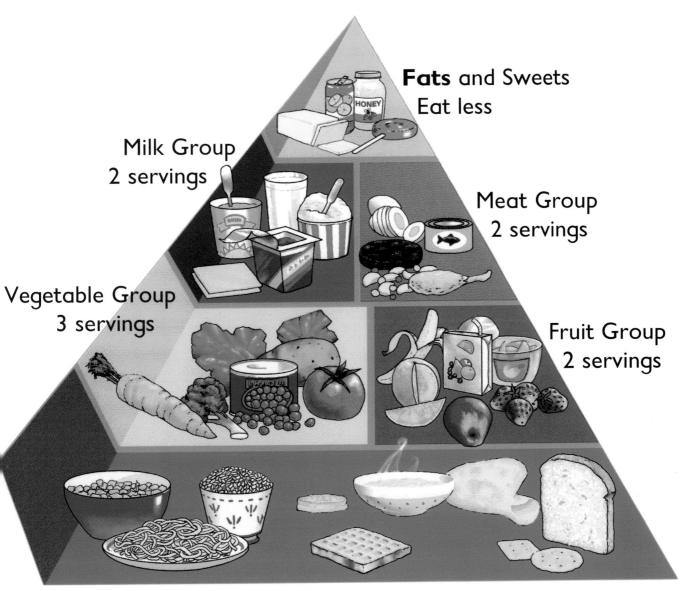

Fats and Sweets
Eat less

Milk Group
2 servings

Meat Group
2 servings

Vegetable Group
3 servings

Fruit Group
2 servings

Grain Group 6 servings

Based on the Food Guide Pyramid for Young Children, U.S. Department of Agriculture, Center for Nutrition Policy and Promotion, March 1999.

27

Vegetable Spread Recipe

1. Peel the carrots and then grate them. Ask an adult to help you do this with a hand grater or in a food processor.

You will need:
- 2 carrots
- 1 zucchini
- 8 oz (200 g) cream cheese
- 1 small bunch of parsley
- pepper

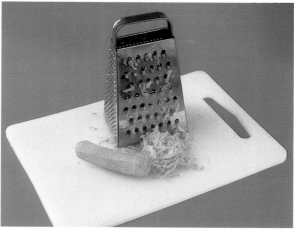

2. Now grate the zucchini in the same way. You do not need to peel it first.

3. Put the grated carrot and zucchini into a bowl with the cream cheese.

4. Chop the parsley carefully and mix it in with the other things. Add a little pepper as well, if you like it.

5. Put the bowl in a fridge to chill. Then you can eat this spread on crackers, toast, or bagels.

Glossary

Ancient Romans people from Rome who ruled a large part of the world about 2,000 years ago

conveyor belt moving belt that takes things placed on it from one place to another

damage to cause harm to something

disease sickness that can harm plants or animals

export to send something to another country to be sold

fat part of some foods that the body uses to get energy and to keep warm

fiber rough part of a plant that passes through our bodies when we eat it

frozen made to be as cold as ice to keep it fresh

grain seed of a cereal plant

packing house building where vegetables are cleaned, sorted, and packed

pest insect that can damage plants

plow machine that breaks up soil to make it ready for planting seeds

product something that is made to be sold

pyramid shape with a flat bottom and three sides with edges that come to a point

raw not cooked

root plant part that grows down into the ground and takes in water and nutrients from the soil

seed the part of a plant that can grow into a new plant

shoot first stem and leaves of a new plant

vegetable part of a plant that we can eat

vitamin something the body needs to grow and stay healthy

31

More Books to Read

Klingel, Cynthia Fitterer, and Robert B. Noyed. *Vegetables*. Milwaukee: Gareth Stevens Incorporated, 2002.

Royston, Angela. *Eat Well*. Chicago: Heinemann Library, 1999.

Royston, Angela. *How Plants Grow*. Chicago: Heinemann Library, 1999.

Index